Original title:
The Last Fern Standing

Copyright © 2025 Creative Arts Management OÜ
All rights reserved.

Author: Evan Hawthorne
ISBN HARDBACK: 978-1-80581-842-7
ISBN PAPERBACK: 978-1-80581-369-9
ISBN EBOOK: 978-1-80581-842-7

Shadows of Survival

In a garden filled with cheer,
A fern stood bold, nothing to fear.
Others wilted, bowed, and groaned,
But this one danced, and proudly moaned.

It wore a hat made of bright sunbeams,
Stood on one leg, or so it seems.
While others drooped in gloomy rows,
It joined a dance, the weirdo shows.

With critters laughing all around,
It hummed a tune, with flair profound.
While leaking water from its fronds,
It made up songs, it sang of ponds.

Through wind and rain, it waved hello,
A comic act in nature's show.
So here's to leafy buffoons and fun,
In the wild, the laughter's just begun!

A Stand of Silence

In a garden of whispers, one leaf does sway,
It's got all the courage, but not much to say.
While others have fallen, it's dancing alone,
A solo sensation, on a leaf-shaped throne.

The breeze starts to giggle, the sun gives a grin,
This little green fighter wears a proud little pin.
All that remains is a memory of cheer,
The humor of nature likes it quiet here.

The Solitary Defense

A lone little sprout on a hill full of hay,
Defends all of ferns in its own quirky way.
Waving its fronds like a general proud,
Proclaiming, 'I'll stand here, I'll shout it real loud!'

With sunlight above, and the ground looking bare,
It flexes its leaves with a comical flair.
A court of old weeds shaking their heads tight,
Wondering how one could put up such a fight!

One among the Withered

In a patch of the past where the dry leaves do sigh,
  One jolly green friend gives it one last try.
  It tickles the raindrops, it giggles at gloom,
    A brave little leafy, defying the doom.

Surrounded by shadows, it can't help but beam,
Dreaming of sunshine with a humorous theme.
The others might worry, but it takes a stand,
With a wink and a twirl, feeling oh-so grand!

Nature's Final Breath

In the finale of greens, where the laughter has fled,
One fella stays rooted, raising its head.
The moon whispers softly, 'Good job, my dear plant,'
While crickets applaud with a tiny little chant.

Oh, the stories it tells of the heights it has seen,
From fireflies dancing to skies ever green.
With a chuckle it bristles, 'I'm the one left here,'
In the humor of nature, it takes center sphere!

Remains of Resilience

In a garden quite dreary,
Stood a fern in a hurry.
While others turned brown,
It wore a green crown.

With roots in the dirt,
It danced without hurt.
Neighbors would sigh,
"That fern is a spy!"

Sunny days turned to rain,
Yet it laughed at the pain.
While blossoms would pout,
The fern had no doubt.

So here's to the bold,
In green, bright and old.
For when friends disappear,
The fern has no fear.

Fronds Against the Winds of Change

They say winds of change blow,
While the fern steals the show.
It twirls in the breeze,
With grace that would please.

Other plants lost their fling,
But it laughs while they cling.
"A twisty new path,"
It giggles with wrath.

In a world full of fads,
Where panic is had,
The fern winks and sways,
As if it knows ways.

Who needs a new look,
When you're off the hook?
Fronds waving in fun,
This fern's just begun!

Memory of a Green Retreat

In a jungle of gray,
Stands one fern, bold and gay.
It reminisces with glee,
About its friend, the tree.

"How we danced in the sun,
Those days were such fun!
With leaves all aglow,
Now it's just me for show."

When weeds come to tease,
The fern responds with ease.
"Sure, take my spot!
You'll find that I'm not fraught."

So it hums a sweet tune,
Underneath the full moon.
Memories alive,
While its fronds still strive.

One Last Breath of Chlorophyll

Last fern on the block,
As others all rock.
It holds on with cheer,
And gives off a sneer.

With grumpy old leaves,
It pretends to tease.
"See how I stand tall,
While you've all gone small?"

A breeze gives a nod,
To the odds it defied.
Sassy, not shy,
This fern doesn't die!

So here it shall sprout,
And say with a pout,
"I'm too good to fade,
And this plan's well laid!"

Solitude in Green

In the garden, I stand alone,
My friends are weeds, by chance they've grown.
The sun laughs at my leafy fate,
In this patch, I'm the most ornate.

All the flowers blush with pride,
While I wait, they giggle and hide.
The breeze tickles my tender fronds,
As I sway, I'm lost in absconds.

Green is the only color I sport,
While daisies throw a fancy court.
I wear my loneliness like a crown,
As pollen drifts through the vibrant town.

Survivor Among Shadows

Once I thrived in the light's embrace,
Now I dance in the dark, a tricky space.
My fellow greens all ran for the sun,
But I'm the one who's lost and won.

The shadows are my buddies now,
With every sip, I take a bow.
Those bold, bright blooms think they're so cool,
While I sip rain, like a leafy fool.

I crack jokes with the night's cool wind,
While the sunflowers just pretend.
I'm the shadow's resilient star,
The survivor among, near and far.

Leaves of Defiance

Oh, the garden is a riot, you see,
With blossoms showing off, oh so free.
But here I am, a leafy sprite,
In my own way, I'll win the fight.

While roses flaunt their thorny might,
I cover up, but still hold tight.
Each leaf unrolls like a funny tale,
In this green world, I'll never pale.

I laugh at the bugs that dare to munch,
I'll outlast their every single crunch.
In a world of colors, I'm the shout,
Leaves of defiance, here's my clout!

A Single Leaf's Lament

Alone I dangle from this tall tree,
Making friends with the buzzing bee.
The squirrels chatter, call me spare,
But I'm busy, I don't care!

No leafy love, just me in the breeze,
As the others fall, I peek through the trees.
Each gust a giggle, each rustle a cheer,
In this lonely plight, I'll persevere.

For when the storms begin to rant,
I'll kick and sway, just like I chant.
With laughter's echo in my spine,
A single leaf, but feeling fine!

The Last Leaf's Lament

Oh, I'm the final leaf, you see,
Hanging on so desperately.
The branches shake, the wind does howl,
I cling on tight, I'm such a fowl!

The squirrels laugh, they dance around,
While I just wish to touch the ground.
"Fall already!" I start to scream,
But here I am, a leaf in dream.

The world keeps changing, I'm a relic,
A leafy joke, it's quite prophetic.
The sun beats down, it's rather hot,
Yet here I stick, all tied in knots.

So when you stroll beneath the trees,
And look for nature's graceful tease,
Remember me, the last to go,
A leaf with flair and lots of show!

Echoes of Fading Green

In a garden full of vibrant sights,
I stand alone, oh what delights!
The daisies puff, the roses blush,
But here I am, no need to rush.

The daisies mock with their bright faces,
While I just wait in quiet places.
"Join us!" they plead, a tempting scene,
But I'm the ghost of fading green.

With every gust, I quiver and shake,
A lonesome plant in this grand mistake.
The weeds all whisper, "You should flee!"
I chuckle back, "Not quite ready, me!"

So here I sit, a funny sight,
A fading echo, holding tight.
In this green world, a quirky stand,
The last to dance upon this land!

Stubborn Roots in a Changing World

Rooted deep in silly soil,
I wriggle around, just to spoil.
The grass around me wants to play,
But I just sit, come what may.

The seasons change, and yet I smile,
Remain an oddball, all the while.
"Just wave goodbye!" the flowers cheer,
But I'm a stubborn root—never fear!

I sip the raindrops, what a treat,
While daisies dance on wobbly feet.
"We're free!" they sing, a wild parade,
But I'm here baking, roots all laid.

So raise a glass, let's toast my cheer,
To the roots that cling, to the leaves that leer.
In this changing world, I make no fuss,
Just a rooted laugh, why not discuss?

A Single Frond's Journey

A single frond, I'm all alone,
On a quest to find my leafy throne.
The wind it whispers, "Go and roam!"
But here I am, so far from home.

I wave to bees, and plead to rats,
"Take me somewhere, with marigold hats!"
They buzz and giggle, "We've got a plan!"
But I'm stuck here, just me and the sand.

Through bustling fields and gardens wide,
I've charmed the bugs, I've swayed with pride.
"Let's take a trip!" the blossoms shout,
But with a laugh, I spin about.

So if you see me, don't you fret,
A single frond, quite the duet.
On this journey, I may be slow,
But with each wiggle, I steal the show!

The Solitary Symphony

In a patch where others fled,
A fern sang its solo instead.
"I'm plantastic!" it declared,
While the daisies just stared.

With a shimmy and a sway,
It danced through the day.
"Who needs a crowd?" it would quip,
"I'm my own membership trip!"

Thorns and Triumphs

In a garden of blooms and thorns,
A lone fern flexed its fawns.
"Who needs roses to vie?
I'll shine, oh my, oh my!"

With thorns nipping near its toes,
"Fear not!" the brave fern chose.
"I'm tough as they come, have you seen?
I've got leaves in the ring, I'm the queen!"

Resilience in the Withering

Amidst a rotting parade,
The fern chuckled, unafraid.
"Watch me thrive like a champ,
While others feel damp!"

As petals wilted in fuss,
"It's just me and the bus!
I'll sprout with a grin, don't you see?
No worries, just smiles, that's my decree!"

An Unseen Struggle

In shadows where sunlight played,
A fern plotted, unafraid.
"Who says I'm lost in the dark?
My humor's a spark!"

With sneaky roots digging wide,
It took broccoli for a ride.
"Fear not, my leafy chums!
I'll lead this fun circus, here it comes!"

Shadows of Abandonment

In a garden where weeds hold court,
The ferns play hide-and-seek for sport.
Dusty leaves and a wink of green,
Laughing at the sunlight's sheen.

They whisper tales of old, long gone,
Of visitors who'd hum a song.
But now they chuckle with dry jokes,
Like old friends sharing quirky pokes.

Underneath the cobweb's lace,
One brave sprout claims this wild place.
With roots that tickle and leaves so bright,
They're dancing in the fading light.

So if you wander to this spot,
Just know that laughter fills the lot.
Among the grandest tales of yore,
The ferns hold court forevermore.

Solitude Among the Foliage

In a forest so silent and deep,
One lonely fern can't find any sleep.
It stretches out for a friendly shout,
But the trees just shrug—what's that about?

Leaves quiver gently in the breeze,
Sharing punchlines with the buzzing bees.
A squirrel giggles at the ferns' plight,
As shadows settle, fading from sight.

The moss rolls its eyes, unimpressed,
While old stones consider them guests.
Roots tangle up in a quirky dance,
Hoping to get that one fern a chance.

A whimsy of greens beneath the sky,
Each one wondering how and why.
In a world where laughter might sprout,
For no reason, they sing and shout.

The Tenacity of Green

In a crack of sidewalk, so bold and spry,
A little fern dares to touch the sky.
Dodging the footfalls and the frowning eyes,
It waves as the passersby hurry and fly.

With a wink and a nudge, it takes a stand,
Throwing leafy shade at the pavement so bland.
Each blade a comedian, cracking a joke,
While pigeons caw and the onlookers choke.

"Look at me, thriving while you just whine,
In this urban jungle, I'm on cloud nine!"
A riot of green, no longer shy,
With friends made of gravel, it aims for the sky.

So here's to the ferns, the jesters of green,
Who find ways to smile when the world's ever mean.
In a concrete cosmos where they don't fit,
They thrive with a spirit that never will quit.

Hope in a Deserted Glade

In a glade where silence swells,
A fern spins stories no one tells.
It tucks in whispers of sunshine bright,
While shadows play in the fading light.

With each gentle curl, it dreams of fun,
While crickets join in, one by one.
"Where did they all go?" chirps a plucky ant,
The fern just shrugs, "Wherever they plant!"

A deer stumbles in with a curious glance,
Finding a place for an impromptu dance.
"Come join us!" calls the fern with glee,
But the deer is timid, and would rather flee.

Yet in the magic of that green heart,
Is laughter that no one can tear apart.
For even alone, there's cheer to be found,
In the laughter of leaves, life abounds.

In the Face of Oblivion

In a world of noisy weeds,
A lone twig stands with pride.
Dancing in the summer breeze,
It claims, 'I will not hide!

Neighbors laugh and poke their fun,
"Look at that silly plant!"
But slowly, surely, one by one,
Those jokers throw a rant.

Leaves like tiny green umbrellas,
Draped in morning dew,
Who knew that tiny fella,
Would outlast all of you?

So here's to the stubborn chap,
Waving cheeky in the sun,
While others take a leafy nap,
It outlasts everyone!

The Quiet Resurgence

Once there was a garden lush,
Where blooms would strut and preen.
But in the quiet, born from hush,
A phantom fern turned green.

While daisies flaunted every hue,
And roses made a fuss,
The fern just smiled and made it through,
In quiet, steadfast trust.

When blooms began to lose their game,
And petals fell like tears,
The fern, it chuckled, quite the same,
"I'm just getting through the years!"

So while the party plants might fade,
And wishes turn to dust,
That fern stands vibrant, unafraid,
With roots, it surely must!

Tendrils of Survival

In cracks of concrete, hope is found,
A tenacious leafy sprout.
Where others may not want to drown,
It wiggles and twists about.

It tickles toes of passersby,
Who laugh and shake their heads.
"Look at that odd little guy!"
"Guess he's got some threads!"

With tiny curls that catch the light,
Each tendril tells a tale,
Of battles fought with all its might,
While others start to pale.

So when you stop and take a glance,
At life where you might roam,
Remember that each little dance,
Might lead a fern back home!

A Testament of Green

In a field where flowers boast,
A single fern stands tall.
With a quirky little post,
Saying, "I'm not small at all!"

The daisies roll their eyes so wide,
While the roses strut and flounce.
But with each gust and playful ride,
The fern stands firm, no doubt!

Who knew it could survive the jest,
The cracks and munch of bugs?
But here it sits, a leafy guest,
Holding on like shrugs.

So let the blooms all raise their glass,
To the stubborn, silly green!
For in this battle, it will surpass,
And reign as the unseen!

Beauty in the Desolate

In a garden of weeds, one plant does a dance,
With the grace of a chicken, it takes every chance.
A sunbeam spots it, a spotlight of fate,
It winks at the daisies, "I'm here, isn't that great?"

With petals a little too ragged and torn,
It twirls in the breeze, all tattered, not worn.
A bug stops for coffee, and laughs at the show,
"Who knew you'd be here, with this grand garden glow?"

When life gives you thorns, just dance with a cheer,
This green little warrior has nothing to fear.
Rooted in chaos, it's the queen of bizarre,
A jester in green with a heart as a star!

So when all seems lost, keep your humor in sight,
In the wildest of places, find joy and delight.
The weeds may encroach, but it stands with a grin,
A symbol of laughter where life can begin!

Remnants of Life

Amidst all the rubble, a sprout claims its space,
Wearing a crown made of dirt on its face.
"Look at me, world!" it shouts out in glee,
While pigeons look on, unimpressed, and flee.

In a cracked sidewalk, a tiny life grows,
It dodges the foot traffic, and everyone knows,
The fate of this plant is a funny old lore,
It thrives near a stash of some old fast-food score.

As night falls around, it takes off its shades,
And throws a wild party, to which no one raids.
With ants as the bouncers and beetles all near,
They dance without worries, no need to adhere.

When thunder starts rumbling, it shimmies and shakes,
"Bring on the deluge! I've got what it takes!"
So here's to the oddballs, the remnants of cheer,
They find joy in a world that's often austere!

Tethered to Existence

A lone little stalk on a treacherous path,
Sways to the rhythm of nature's sly wrath.
"Catch me if you can," it snickers with pride,
While raindrops and insects take on the ride.

With roots intertwined in a mash of good luck,
It ducks through the shadows, "Just try to get stuck!"
A leaflike a banner, it dances in storms,
"Is this an apocalypse? Oh well, it's just norms!"

Among shouting weeds, it huddles and grins,
Visualizing concerts where chaos begins.
"I'll sing with the wind, let the clouds feel my tune,
In this comical chaos, I'll bubble like noon!"

So here's to the ferns, with their antics so bold,
They laugh in the wind as their stories unfold.
In a world full of armor, they shun the charade,
Tethered to laughter, their strength never fades.

A Solitary Remembrance

By the edge of a cliff, a lone leaf does sway,
Recalling the days it once danced in the fray.
"Ah, to be young!" it sighs with a flair,
As echoes of laughter swirl through the air.

Once part of a forest, a bustling bazaar,
Now a quiet solo, a leftover star.
It tells silly stories to beetles that stare,
"Remember the sun? How we soaked up the glare?"

With each gust of wind, it spins tales of old,
Of cousins and friends, their memories bold.
Though time slips away like a feather on breeze,
This leaf stands resilient, doing whatever it please.

"Let others forget," it resolutely beams,
"I'm the whole of the past, wrapped in vibrant dreams."
In solitude's embrace, it struts like a king,
A testament to joy, the heart can still sing!

Heart of the Untamed

In a jungle of leaves, a lone green sprout,
Waving its fronds like it's here to shout.
With a wink and a nod, it dances in glee,
Saying, "Look at me, I'm wild and free!"

While all others fade, it laughs with a twist,
"Are you done? Oh please, I simply insist!"
Winds whisper secrets of glorious fame,
While it delights in its own silly game.

Sunshine beaming, it strikes a bold pose,
Ignoring the ruckus from dirt to the roes.
"Oh, I'm not worried, I'm chubby and stout,
You think I'll fall? Just look at me sprout!"

So raise a glass to this frolicsome shade,
With fronds waving wildly, it won't be swayed.
For in this big world, where most just pretend,
Who needs all the praise when you've got a friend?

In Solitary Bloom

In a pot by the window, one little plant,
Looks at the world with a curious rant.
"Why do they frolic? Why do they race?
I'm happy to sit here, enjoying my space!"

While daisies and roses boast about size,
This cheeky green fella just rolls its bright eyes.
"Go ahead, you fancy blooms, show off your flair,
I'm the zen master of this floral affair!"

Bees come to buzz, but it shrugs and just sighs,
"It's nice having friends, but I'm wise to their lies.
They talk of big gardens, of sunshine and sweat,
But I've got a sunny, laid-back mindset!"

So here in the silence, the rogue does remain,
With its whiskers of green, it's gone quite insane.
Who needs the spotlight when you've got your chill?
In solitary bloom, it's McPlant in the still!

Against the Storm

A tempest was brewing, the skies turning gray,
While the garden went panicking, running away.
But one quirky sprout, with a sparkle and glee,
Just giggled aloud, "It's a fine day for me!"

Raindrops were falling, like drummers on kits,
Yet our sprightly green buddy just danced through the fits.

"Oh, bring on the thunder! I'll sway and I'll spin,
These drops are just kisses—I'm ready to win!"

While others were bending, breaking in fright,
This sprout stood up tall, with all of its might.
"Hail? Oh, pish posh! I'm built like a tank,
You think I will buckle? Well, what do you think?"

And as skies cleared up and the sun shone in rays,
This jubilant sprout had the best of the days.
So here's to the cheer, the fun in the shambles,
For those few sweet plants who just love their rambles!

Verdant Outlast

In a garden of glory where flowers all cheer,
There's a small spry green fellow who's anything but sheer.
"Are you all glamoured up? Well, look at me shine!
I'm a rugged survivor, and I'm feeling just fine!"

When petals are wilting and fragrance is gone,
This daring green sprout rises at dawn.
"I don't need the colors, the dazzling display,
For nature's my canvas, I'm here to stay!"

While daisies are pouting and lilies in bloom,
The sprout takes a bow in the garden's big room.
"Cheers to the leaves that don't need to compete,
I'm the punchline of life, and oh-so sweet!"

So here's to the green with its comical flair,
No grandiose petals, but it doesn't care.
With laughter and leaves, it will always outlast,
For those who embrace every quirky contrast!

Verdancy's Last Stand

In a forest devoid of glee,
One lone leaf swayed in the breeze.
All its friends had taken flight,
Leaving it to face the night.

It waved to a butterfly, true,
'Hey there, can I join you too?'
But the butterfly just laughed and fled,
Leaving our fern to scratch its head.

With no plants to chat and confide,
It made a pact with a fallen pine.
They shared stories of years gone by,
While dreaming of the lush nearby.

Oh how it wished for a dance,
To sway with more than just chance.
But all it could do was stand,
Pointing to clouds, quite unplanned.

Solitude in the Wild

In a jungle of chatter and cheer,
Stood a fern with no friends near.
It tried to joke with a passing beetle,
But the beetle just thought it a riddle.

It stretched its fronds, a sight to see,
And said, 'Oh come, dance with me!'
But the beetle just snickered and sped,
Leaving the fern feeling quite misled.

A wise old rabbit peeked from a bush,
'Life's too short for this silly hush!'
And soon they formed a quirky duo,
With antics that would steal the show.

Together they laughed at the world with glee,
A fern and a rabbit, wild and free.
In solitude, they found a bond,
Two oddballs, forever fond.

Secrets of the Long-Living

Amidst the wise, old, towering trees,
A fern held secrets on its leaves.
Wondering how to keep its glow,
While others around it started to slow.

It whispered to worms and ants at play,
'What's the trick to livin' each day?'
They chuckled back, 'Just soak up the sun,
And maybe some jokes would be fun!'

So it started telling tales of old,
Of adventures daring and bold.
Other plants would gather and squeal,
As the fern spun yarns, what a deal!

Years passed, and the fern stood proud,
With laughter echoing, its heart loud.
In each secret, it found its pride,
An old fern, with joy as its guide.

A Life Left Behind

Once sprouted in a vibrant patch,
A fern thought life was quite the catch.
But leaves turned brown and fell away,
As memories hung like a disarray.

Old boots were tossed, a hat went missing,
'Hey folks, come back! You're really dissing!'
But its cry echoed through quiet air,
No one heard its plight or care.

It played charades with rocks and stones,
Telling tales in funny tones.
Oh, how it wished for just one friend,
To laugh together 'til the end.

With vines of laughter, it devised a plan,
To throw a bash for an old tin can.
Alone it stood, yet so alive,
In a world where joy could still thrive.

Against Time and Tide

In the garden where others wilt,
Stands a sprout, proud without guilt.
Time and tide wash all away,
Yet this green persists, come what may.

Weathered storms and harsh sun rays,
It nods its head in quirky ways.
A dance with gusts that try to tease,
This little plant won't bend with ease.

Roots sunk deep, it hugs the ground,
With every laugh, it makes a sound.
While others pout, it strikes a pose,
A champion where no one knows.

So raise a glass, give it a cheer,
For the sassy fern without a fear.
Against the odds, it will survive,
With leafy laughter, it will thrive.

The Defiant Green

In a pot amidst the dreary night,
A little leaf gave us a fright.
With a wink and a smile so sly,
It proclaimed, 'Not yet! I won't die!'

While others droop and hang their heads,
This feisty fern loves to make beds.
'Take your gloom and send it away,
I'm just getting started—let's play!'

Beneath the light, it does a jig,
With every gust, it does a gig.
Daring squirrels and pesky bugs,
It throws them all some playful shrugs.

Who knew a plant could have such zest?
In the garden of gloom, it's truly blessed.
A tale of joy among the weeds,
That cheeky fern fulfills our needs.

Roots of Tenacity

Deep in the soil where antics dwell,
A spritely fern has tales to tell.
With roots that laugh at obstacles high,
In a world of frowns, how could it cry?

Beneath the moon, it strikes a pose,
With drapes of green that twist and pose.
As weeds roll by, it gives a wink,
Watch out, world, it's time to think!

Tiny critters munching near,
Can't touch this plant; it gives a cheer.
'Grumpy greens will take a hike,
I'm the king; let's ride a bike!'

So if you see it, doff your hat,
To the fern that's having a chat.
Its roots, a testament of glee,
Amongst the sad, it holds the key.

The Unbreakable Canopy

Underneath the great blue sky,
A leafy rebel comes flying by.
With tendrils strong and spirit bold,
It steals the show—just watch it unfold.

Friends with the breeze, it dances true,
While sunbeams play hide-and-seek too.
Twirling swirls of vibrant green,
It's the happiest sight you've ever seen.

From cheeky rains to soggy days,
This leafy comic knows all ways.
With giggles tucked in every frond,
It waves to all—of life we're fond!

A canopy of joy, it proudly beams,
With every inch, it grows our dreams.
So here's to our little spirited friend,
May its laughter and wit never end!

Emblems of Endurance

In a garden once so bright,
The ferns had quite a fright.
One stood proud with leafy grace,
While others vanished without a trace.

"I'm the champion!" it clung to pride,
While companions took their final slide.
Its fronds waved like a silly flag,
In a landscape where all would brag.

Sprinklers drip and squirrels pretzel,
'Who knew ferns could be so metal?'
Raccoons chuckle from afar,
While Luna the cat blames it on the jar.

But nature's games are oh-so-funny,
When your pals disappear, isn't it punny?
One solo frond dancing in glee,
While all around is a big empty spree.

The Green Unknown

Underneath shadows of ancient trees,
A single fawn creeps with the breeze.
"What's this?" it wonders, eyes so wide,
As it spots the fern with a quirky stride.

The fawn pokes it with a hoofy poke,
Is it real or just a joke?
The fern wobbles, it giggles, it bends,
And whispers, "I've outlasted all my friends!"

Bright sun shines down, what a scene!
A dazzling style, so fresh and green!
"You're weird!" said the fawn, with a huff,
But the fern just giggled, "Well, that's tough!"

Together they made quite a pair,
In the realm of foliage, beyond compare.
One had roots, the other, big hopes,
A fern and a fawn, both full of gropes.

Remembrance on Barren Soil

Amidst the ruins, a greenish glow,
One lone sprout putting on a show.
"How did you stay?" the dust asked shy,
"While all others waved their sad goodbye!"

With a chuckle, the sprout twirled around,
"I'm the stubborn one, the talk of the ground!"
In the land of the forgotten boo,
It sprouted stories, both bright and blue.

Whispers of wind carried the tales,
Of friends who once danced on green trails.
While they turned to mulch, consumed by the floor,
Our sprout just laughed, wanting more lore.

"Put up your feet, and let's reminisce!"
It declared with a tilt, offering bliss.
"In sadder times, I bloom and smile,
So gather round, let's laugh for a while!"

A Beacon Amidst Ruins

On a crumbled wall where ivy sprawls,
A fern does a frolic, defying all calls.
"I'm here to stay," it dances with flair,
Mocking the cacti and moss in despair.

As if saying, "Look, this is my show!"
It sways with vigor, putting on quite a flow.
"While you lose your battles from drought's cruel kiss,
I nap under sunshine; I just can't miss!"

A squirrel stops to take a gander,
"You're ridiculous, tell me... what's your brand, dear?"
"I'm brand new! Just faking my plight,
Living off laughter, day and night!"

So when you glimpse the last of the greens,
Remember the giggle, chase away the beans.
Even in ruins, there's joy to be found,
A fern with a pun, forever unbound.

An Ode to Endurance

In a garden so bright, all plants did thrive,
One little fern took a dive.
While daisies danced in the warm, sweet air,
This lone guy clung with a quirky flair.

As petunias giggled, and daisies twirled,
Our fern just smiled, unfurled and twirled.
With roots so sturdy, it laughed at the rain,
Saying, 'Bring on the drought, bring on the pain!'

Dealing with weeds, who ruled with force,
Our fern stood firm, a fun little horse.
Swaying to wind with a comedic jig,
While other plants learned to dance a big gig.

So here's to the fern, both brave and spry,
A master of jest, reaching for the sky.
In patchy sunlight, it finds its beat,
Oh, fern friend, you can't be beat!

Spirits Amongst the Withered

When all else has wilted, and stems have gone sad,
Our fern still chuckles, the cheeky little lad.
With leaves like a wig, it doesn't mind gloom,
A spirit of mischief, it fills up the room.

Amongst fading roses and drooping old thyme,
It whispers sweet jokes as if clocking in time.
While others decay in their garden regret,
This fern stays afloat, with no hint of fret.

It teases the daisies, who blush with their shame,
Saying, "I'm still here, while you play the blame!"
The sun may be shy, but it laughs and it beams,
Growing amidst all the "beings" of dreams.

So let's raise a toast to the fern, and its jest,
In a world full of wilt, it's truly the best.
A spirit of laughter, forever set free,
Rooted in joy, oh, so playfully!

Remnant of a Green Dream

In the realm of decay, where green fades away,
A lone fern pops up, with a grin for the day.
While flowers lay flat, and leaves sigh in pain,
This sprightly little guy probes the sun with disdain.

"I'll outlast the drought, I'll outshine the bloom,
A relic of hope, in a garden of gloom!"
It shakes off the dust, does a little dance,
"As long as you water, I'll take my chance!"

Amongst wilting lilies and petals forlorn,
Our fern finds delight, though the others all mourn.
It smiles at the chaos, with roots like a joke,
Saying, "I'm not crazy, I'm just broke!"

So here's to the fern, the dream that won't die,
With a knack for survival, oh me, oh my!
Clinging to laughter, it's green and it beams,
A remnant of joy, stemming from dreams!

Branches of Fate

In a world of perishing roots and dry leaves,
Stands one little fern, bright as it believes.
"While trees take a nap and the shrubs play a game,
I'll keep on my dance, my fern-loving fame!"

Beneath weathered branches, where shadows fall thick,
The fern learns to stand firm, oh isn't that slick?
With a wink to the moon and a nod to the sun,
It prances with glee, saying, "Look at me run!"

As violets frown and the grass feels old,
Our fern shimmies proudly, so bold and so gold.
"Do you hear all the whispers of branches that sway?
They think I'm a joke, but I'm here to stay!"

So let's cheer for the fern, in its leafy bright fate,
For laughing in storms, it's truly first-rate.
A branch of resilience, with humor that's great,
In the garden of life, it dances, sedate!

Verdant Survivor

In a garden full of weeds,
One green sprout stands tall,
With a wink and a nod,
Saying, "Not today, y'all!"

While daisies roll their eyes,
And dandelions pout,
This little leafy fella,
Knows what it's about!

Dancing in the sunlight,
With ferny grace,
While others flee and cower,
It claims its happy space.

Oh, what a bouncy sprout
With roots so deep and wide,
Who knew surviving here
Could be such a fun ride!

Embrace of the Forgotten

In an old and shady nook,
Where shadows stretch and droop,
A fern with quirky leaves
Hosts a grumpy toad troupe.

They grunt and croak all day,
In their leafy green chair,
While ferns just giggle softly,
"You think you're so rare!"

Unbothered by their noise,
Our fern just sways and sighs,
Drawing laughter from the past
And whispering old lies.

The breeze gives them a shove,
They huff and puff in vain,
But the fern just beams and winks
As they complain again.

The Lonesome Lunge

Once there was a fern alone,
With no friend in sight,
It did a little dance,
In the pale moonlight.

It lunged towards the daisies,
And tripped on a stone,
They laughed till they were hollow,
"Oh, you're all on your own!"

Yet unfazed by their glee,
It struck a pose so grand,
Hollering to the night sky,
"I'll still make my stand!"

With each clumsy lunge,
It found its rhythm bold,
Because who needs a buddy,
When you're fern-ish and gold?

Fragments of a Dying Glade

In a meadow once so grand,
With colors bright and bold,
Now sits a shady fern,
With tales yet untold.

The grass is laughing sideways,
While twigs begin to break,
But our fern just shakes its head,
And giggles at the shake.

"This dying glade's a twist,
A plot with all the turns,
But every leaf that tumbles,
A new fun-fact it earns!"

So here it stands, delighted,
With time to sip some tea,
In the fragments of a glade,
Where all is wild and free!

Against the Dying Light

In a quirky glade where shadows play,
A green friend stands, come what may.
With leaves like hands, waving goodnight,
Saying, "I'm here! Let's win this fight!"

Bending under the sun's bright glare,
It whispers jokes to the timid hare.
"Why did the shrub cross the dirt path?"
To escape a gardener's wicked wrath!

Chasing off weeds with a flick and a twist,
"Do you really think I'll be missed?"
A frilly fern with cosmic flair,
Twirling in breezes like it don't care!

So laugh with the leaves, let worries go,
Raise a toast to ferns and their fierce show.
In twilight's dance, their humor ignites,
Fun never tires, against dying lights.

The Lone Green Sentinel

One fern's quite bold, all on its own,
In a world where the flowers have overgrown.
"Whatcha looking at?" it cheekily grins,
As daisies roll their eyes, toss their pins!

The woodland critters stop and stare,
"Can't we all just get somewhere?"
Yet the fern stands tall, dressed in green,
Sassy and proud, a true evergreen!

With roots in the ground and head held high,
"Not everyone's meant for the sky!"
Making jokes with the passing breeze,
Says, "I'm not just any plant, I'm a tease!"

So cheer for the fern, the solo champ,
Brightened the shade with its private lamp.
While others fade, it laughs with delight,
The lone green watcher, in the cool night.

Fragments of a Forgotten Forest

In a forest lost to the sands of time,
A fern's life is pure, but also a crime.
"I'm too cool for thickets!" it proudly brags,
While hidden bears watch, wearing rags.

Once a thriving gang of leafy pals,
Now just memories and fairy tales.
"I'm the last laugh in this spooky show!"
It quips with pride, ready to glow!

Sprouting quirky jokes on each fern frond,
Trading gossip with squirrels so fond.
"Why did the leaf never go away?"
It just couldn't find a sunniest day!

Fragments of laughter dance in the mist,
A lone fern winks, and you can't resist.
Echoes of joy from a forest once bright,
Still remain, in the fading light.

Unyielding Flora

In the wilds where wild things roam,
There's one sprightly fern that calls it home.
"I'll never yield!" it chants with glee,
"I'm built to last as you can see!"

With roots like anchors, strong and proud,
It hosts a party for the wandering crowd.
"Care for a sip from my dew drop cup?"
It laughs and dances, never gives up!

When rain clouds grumble, it gives a wink,
"I thrive in the damp! Just take a drink!"
It cracks a joke with the cloudy weather,
"Who needs a roof when we're all together?"

So tip your hat to this feisty delight,
A fern with attitude, ready to fight.
With humor and heart, it stands with might,
In a world that dims, it shines so bright!

Fading Echoes

In a forest, once lush and bright,
A plant holds on, ready to fight.
Its friends have gone, what a scene!
The last of a party, oh so keen!

With a twist and a turn, it sways,
In a dance of survival, it plays.
Mossy whispers try to distract,
But it chuckles back, undeterred, intact!

A squirrel stops by, gives a cheer,
"You're the greenest one left, hold dear!"
Lonely it may seem, yet it grins,
A botanical king, where life begins!

All the other plants, what a fuss,
Maybe they're lost, or riding a bus.
But this fern stands firm, quite the charmer,
Waving to the wind, not a heavy drama!

Last Blooms

In a garden where flowers once bloomed,
A lone stem stands, all together doomed.
"Where did you go?" it starts to speak,
To petals that fluttered, now so meek.

Butterflies stop, doing a double take,
"Is that a fern? It's no piece of cake!"
The fern replies with a cheeky grin,
"I'm the headliner here; wanna join in?"

A weed pokes its head in pure surprise,
"You're still standing? Man, that's wise!"
The fern puffs up, all prissy and proud,
Says, "I only hang with the brave and loud!"

Its glory days filled with sunshine and shade,
But it won't give up—not on this parade.
With laughter and mirth, it dances in style,
While the others reminisce for a while!

The Forgotten Tapestry

Once a forest, a textile of green,
But now just one fern, looking quite mean.
"You might have left, but I'm still here,"
Proclaims the lone plant, full of cheer.

Vines twist and twine, in a vain attempt,
To recall what was; it's a plant's lament.
The fern laughs out loud, "Is this a trick?"
"You think you can top my green magic?"

A rabbit hops by with a quizzical stare,
"What's with the one-plant show? Quite rare!"
"Join me, my friend! It's a long, fun ride,
On this last leaf ship, we'll float with pride!"

So they gather round, quite the makeshift crew,
A patchwork of life, nothing new.
While forgotten tapestries may tend to fade,
This fern still dances, undismayed!

Lingering in the Ruins

In a garden that crumbled, but still looked grand,
A fern stands proud, defying the land.
"What happened here?" it loudly muses,
"Am I a relic? Or have I fused?"

With bricks all around, and weeds in despair,
The fern strikes a pose, with flair and care.
"A quirky old ruin, that's what I see!"
"Oh, come join my party! Just you and me!"

A crow caws out, perched high and wise,
"Dear fern, your humor is quite the surprise!"
"I may be one, but I'm far from dull,
With every joke, I'm the sparkling jewel!"

So as the days fade, and seasons may shift,
The fern stays vibrant, a humorous gift.
Lingering in ruins, where laughter resounds,
It rules all it surveys, in playful bounds!

The Green Hero

In a kingdom of green, where plants should thrive,
Stands a fern who claims, "I'm still alive!"
While daisies wilt and the petals fall,
It stands as a beacon, answering the call.

With the weeds all whining, and bushes a mess,
The fern pulls a cape made of grass, no less!
"Fear not, dear friends, I'm here to defend,
This party of foliage, until the end!"

A breeze carries whispers, the sun shines bright,
The fern spins around, in a heroic light.
"Let's dance through the drought, we shall not yield,
For laughter's the armor of our green field!"

So it leads the way, with a hop and a twirl,
Every rustling leaf, it manages to hurl.
A funny green hero, with valor it gleams,
In a world of plants, it reigns with dreams!

Whispers of the Evergreen

In the forest, a green prankster,
Making friends with a wandering tree.
Telling jokes to a squirrel so cute,
While moss giggles and starts to agree.

Leaves are laughing in the breezy air,
Crickets chirp in a harmony fair.
The branches sway, doing a dance,
Nature's comedy, a funny romance.

A raccoon pops in for a casual peek,
"Can I join in? I'm a comedian freak!"
The trees all chuckle, the sky rolls its eyes,
While the ferns plot their pranks, oh what a surprise!

Laughter echoes through the glade,
A band of flora, in joy they parade.
With roots entwined and spirits so spry,
In the heart of greens, the whimsy won't die.

Solitary Petals in the Twilight

A lonely bloom in a crowded field,
Stands tall, with flair, its fate revealed.
Whispering secrets to the buzzing bees,
It chuckles softly, teasing the breeze.

"Why do all daisies have such big dreams?
When I am the star, or so it seems!"
With petals so vibrant, it struts about,
In the twilight glow, without a doubt.

Even the shadows start to align,
To hear this flower's witty design.
A poppy winks, "You're quite the catch!"
Together they giggle, a perfect match.

As night descends, it bows with grace,
While stars twinkle, joining the race.
A solitary petal, but never alone,
In twilight's laughter, it's found a home.

Resilience Beneath the Canopy

In the shade where sunlight barely creeps,
A fern in a corner giggles and leaps.
"Who needs the sun? I'm thriving in style!
Dancing with raindrops, oh, what a while!"

The trees around whisper tales of fun,
Of brave little warriors, not seeking the sun.
"Why worry of drought? I'm green all year,
With humor as armor, I've nothing to fear!"

A turtle strolls past with a puzzled grin,
"Are you growing after all this din?"
"Oh dear friend," the fern winks with cheer,
"With laughter and joy, I'm the ruler here!"

Beneath the big leaves, a party begins,
All critters gather, sharing their wins.
For resilience grows when laughter takes root,
Beneath this green canopy, there's always a suit.

Alone Among the Shadows

A lone trunk stretches, in dark hues it blends,
While whispers of jokes from the canopy sends.
"Did you hear the one about shadows that play?
They trip on the light, then just fade away!"

Underneath, where the ferns like to scoot,
A cheeky little sprout gives a grand hoot.
"I may seem alone, but don't be misled,
I'm the queen of this shadow, I'm well overfed!"

Mushrooms giggle, they sprout from below,
Joining the laughter in the soft, gentle glow.
"Don't count me out just because I'm small,
I'm the jester of gloom, I amuse one and all!"

So here in the dusk, where light softly sighs,
The ferns and their friends plot their sweet little lies.
With humor as shelter, they'll welcome the night,
Alone among shadows, they're ready to write.

Guardian of a Deserted Glade

In the quiet glen, one plant stands tall,
Cracked as a joke, yet proud through it all.
Leaves like confetti, in muted green hue,
Waving with laughter, the whole wide view.

Squirrels pass by, with a curious glance,
This lonely green buddy dares to dance.
Twirling in breezes, head held up high,
"I'm the king of this place!" it shouts to the sky.

Beneath golden sun, it basks with delight,
No time for sadness, just pure, silly flight.
Others have withered, but it finds a way,
As it plots wild parties each bright sunny day.

With the moon as its witness, it sways and it spins,
In this ferny world, it knows it always wins.
So raise up a toast, with a smile and cheer,
To the guardian plant that will never disappear!

Emergence from Ashes

From ashes and ruins, a sprout can be found,
With a cheeky green grin, it's the lone stand-around.
"Survivor's my game, and I play it just right,"
It braves the odd winds that come on a night.

While flowers all sigh, in their colors so bright,
This little green joker takes on every fright.
With roots in the ground, and a wink in its leaf,
It giggles at doom, oh what a belief!

"Why wilt and why wilt when you can just sass?"
It teases the clouds with a twirl and a pass.
While others fall down, with their petals all torn,
This sprightly oddity just laughs and stays sworn.

So gather around for the bonkers delight,
It's a leafy spectacle—a tease in the night.
For from the old cinders, new life finds its route,
With a wink and a dance, it's the fae sprout about!

Portrait of One Resilience

A single green hero on a tilt of a stone,
Tells stories of grit, though its voice is a drone.
"Woe is my motif, but oh, what a twist!"
Every wilt that I've weathered has turned into bliss.

With laughter and snickers, it rolls with the times,
Adding a spark to the dullest of climes.
"I wore wounds like gold, if pain could be art!"
Now it struts like a peacock, proud of its heart.

While others just sulk in the shadows of fate,
This fern shines like fireworks, never too late.
It whispers to critters as they come and go,
"We're all just survivors, enjoying the show!"

So here's to the fern, with a wink and a cheer,
Life's a funny dance, when you stay in the clear.
With roots deep and branches that catch every smile,
In the gallery of weeds, it stands all the while!

Stalwart in Sorrow

In the heart of the gloom, one leaf gives a grin,
A stalwart green wonder, beneath thick, tangled skin.
With a nod to the troubles that life leaves in tow,
It chuckles-soft whispers, "Oh, where else to grow?"

Surrounded by frowns, in a monotone sea,
This quirky green warrior finds joy, wild and free.
"While others may wilt, I'll dance through the tears,
Unfazed by the rain, I fashion my cheers!"

Each droplet's a drummer, that sings to its tune,
"Join me, oh friends, under the light of the moon!"
It fluffs up its fronds, with a cheeky little jeer,
"Let's make a parade, let's banish all fear!"

So wave to the fern, in vibrant retreat,
For sorrow's just spice in this wild life so sweet.
In the tapestry woven of giggles and sighs,
The steadfast green jest comes alive in disguise!

www.ingramcontent.com/pod-product-compliance
Lightning Source LLC
Chambersburg PA
CBHW070334120526
44590CB00017B/2882